AF406277

Poetry of
Life Love and Loss

CAROL LYNN CASWELL

Acknowledgement

This book would not have been completed without the technical and artistic assistance of Craig Birklid and Stacey Caswell. I feel fortunate to have Stacey and Craig in my life. Thank you both so much for your inspiration and help as this book moved along to completion.

About The Author

Carol Lynn Caswell is from the Pacific Northwest. She attended Franklin Pierce High School and Pacific Lutheran University. She was an editor of her high school and college newspapers. She has a Bachelor's Degree in Social Work from PLU, a Bachelor of Science from Weber State in Ogden, Utah, and a Master's Degree in English from William Patterson University in Wayne, New Jersey. She has always loved to write and according to one high school teacher has a gift for writing. Carol was a social worker, a teacher, a college instructor, and she retired from the Washington State Labor and Industries as coordinator of Private Rehabilitation Services , during which time she wrote and edited a newsletter to all people treating clients from Washington state Labor and Industries, including doctors and rehab workers in other countries.

Before and after retirement she traveled to Europe a few times, Hawaii many times, and China once. She maintained a home in Mesa Arizona for 25 years for the winter months, enjoying the sunshine, activities and friends there. She published a previous book in 2003.

Carol Lynn has three sons, one granddaughter, five grandsons and one great grandson.

Table of Contents

Acknowledgement	*3*
About The Author	*4*
A Child	*7*
Autumn Hymn	*9*
Do You Recall	*11*
Friend	*13*
Highway Life	*15*
I Will Remember	*17*
Let Me Touch You	*19*
Renouncement	*21*
Return	*23*
Spring Morning	*25*
Summer Storm	*27*
The New House	*29*
The Perfect Day	*31*
The Trap Of Time	*33*
Unborn Child	*35*
Vietnam 1975	*37*
You And Me	*39*

A Child

But the baby had black hair,
The baby wasn't fair.
Its head was covered in long, black hair.
Whose baby is that there?
The one with the ebony hair.
The shiny, satin strands are woven in a crown.
A wreath of dark gold, pure refined.
Who made that baby's hair?
What bursting love has flowered here
To live, to mark the place where love has been.

Autumn Hymn

Pumpkins lie like
Golden moons fallen from October skies,
Tired cornstalks prop each other up to whisper in the wind.
Bleeding leaves drip to a gentle earthen grave.
It is autumn.
I live again when summer dies.

Do You Recall

Do you recall at all
How it blossomed in the spring?
How the green-thrilled garment
That we wound around us tight
Seemed to burst with the ripe
Fragrant flowers?
Do you recall at all?

Did you notice when the wind
Kissed a blue-cooled wave?
We went sliding down the bank
Hit the grit with a gray velvet hurt.
Did you notice when it hurt?

Were your eyes wise
When a brown-chilled day
Split an oak on its way
To a storm?

In the winter of my mind,
My love,
Are you skipping in the sun?

Friend

One of the beautiful things that I see
When I think of your life in relation to me,
Is the way that you listen to small things I say,
Is the glow of your smile when your eyes look my way.

And in giving you pleasure I find
Don't you see?
That the greatest of pleasure returns
Back to me!

Highway Life

Hum pulling, gear straining
Trucks cascade swiftly over
The stretching tar.
Streaming yellow streaks chase the distance.
Passing, passing
Lull and roar
Whine and whiz,
Snug cubicles of time,
A moving womb.
The pull of power piercing the maiden air.
A hurried trip to anywhere,
A blink of time,
The mini-death of arrival
Sleeps alone
Until the next encounter.

I Will Remember

I will remember.
There will be a quiet point,
A particular perception of the eye,
An evocation of the brain,
And the memory of you will
Wash over me like cool waves,
Sifting soft mental fingers
Like sand through my mind,
Dredging the deep tidal pool
Reserved for hidden dreams.
Then my heart will come home to you
And sing a gentle hymn of love.
And I will remember.

Let Me Touch You

Let me touch you, gentle love,
With hands that offer up my soul,
For you,
To drink your fill,
Until
Our hands slip
Out of touch,
And live to breathe in
Minds alone.
Suspended time,
Yours and mine,
Together.

Renouncement

I fling my life into the day,
I heap and mound the daily tasks,
To shore my heart against the tide,
The drowning , longing pull of you.
I set my heart a steady stride.

Sleep the beauty of my soul,
Counting out the dripping days,
The silent, hollow, haunted days.

I loved you then.
Now is the season of renouncement.

Return

I walked along the beach today
And my heart sang low
With a moaning song
To match the screeching of the gulls.

I walked alone on the beach today,
The sand caved down
And rose in mounds
Around my feet,

Soft gray velvet
To lie upon
And dream of other days.

Spring Morning

Clear morning light streaks narrow golden paths across the water.
Cool winds create giant sea monster shadows moving
Swiftly under the surface from shore to shore.
Two ducks beginning in a sudden swim rise together
Moving in tandem harmony.

Would that I could fly with you!
To feel the wind rush past my face,
To view the earth from places high and free.
To sit with you upon a moment in time,
A space of nothing, strong and firm,
To ride with you the vapor trail left
By distant twinkling lights.
To all the earth and out beyond,
To where we really do belong.

Summer Storm

I love to watch a summer storm
Gather in dusky clouds across the lake
Until streaks of lightning slash like
A razor's slice opening the gray wrist of the sky.
The sudden leak of liquid life gushes to the earth.
It falls on grass and streets and trees,
On summer laughter on a bridge.
Taste the rain upon my lips,
Kiss my mingled tears away.
The rain and sadness blend so well.
Which is life and which is death?
I draw your death into my soul
And hold it there until your need shall loose my grasp.
You lit my sky with jagged pain,
Exquisite, flashing bursts of love, mixed with
Raining eyes.

The New House

The saws are singing building songs,
A serenade of rip and tear
Electric music on the air,
Creation's highest call.

A crooning song to woo the wood,
To cut and shape and seal the form,
The saws are singing morning songs,
The dawn of house arises from
The night of barren land.

The saws are singing cutting songs
That wound the wood, to make the shape.
The saws are singing songs of life,
The house will grow complete and strong
Created in the metal song
And then will sing no more.

The Perfect Day

Had I my life to spend with you,
If open-ended time would purr and hum
Stretched into the dawns and darks
Of countless days.

Then slipping, sleeping, floating clear,
Caught together and tossed,
We would pass our days
In wanton praise of love.

On sojourns to exotic lands,
In slumbering villas by the sea,
Beside the hearth, upon your knee
Locale would change but we would be

Would be for always
Reverent in the awe of night,
Blind to the clutch and claim
Of age's toothless, cackle face.

But I have alone
This day for you,
One day select from all the rest,
One pure and perfect casque to fill.

As night rides in with cool dark hands
And ours release
To let us live forever young,
I wonder at the tricks of time.
Have we lived the years or just this one
Perfect day?

The Trap Of Time

I'm tangled in the trap of time,
Rigid unabridged hours
Count and tick and lock
My love away.

Time is passed; time lies ahead,
It haunts the quiet corner of my mind.
Is it time for this or time for that?
Who keeps the score?
It's such a chore.
All the friendships put away,
A new one's coming in today.

Time you've made me rich and poor,
You've hammered home with nails of truth
The shrouded lid of love.

The time is now; the time is dead.
The strings are stretched beyond the ear.
It is the mind alone can hear
The melody of time.

Unborn Child

Run away little girl
In your pale blue dress
Run away, run away from those who love you best.
Keep your freedom sure in the tall tan grass
Hide among the pine trees
Whisper in the wind
Dark eyed laughing child
Moon faced scamp
Wing away across the hill
Peep at me behind the sill
Hands that reach but never touch.
Perhaps I dream a bit too much.

Vietnam 1975

A long look back
At hungry eyes.
At paper promises
That fill the wind
With scattered ashes.
A cry for peace.
A crumpled life
A twisted tarnished, tattered
Prize that cries and cries
And cries.

You And Me

You and me
Can we be
Separate beings,
Caught together
And held apart
By soul's divisions?
Rather blend our souls
As one complete,
In joy and peace.
My love, my soul,
Myself.
My measure of eternity
Is you.

www.ingramcontent.com/pod-product-compliance
Lightning Source LLC
Chambersburg PA
CBHW042045130726
48010CB00024B/206